NO

C

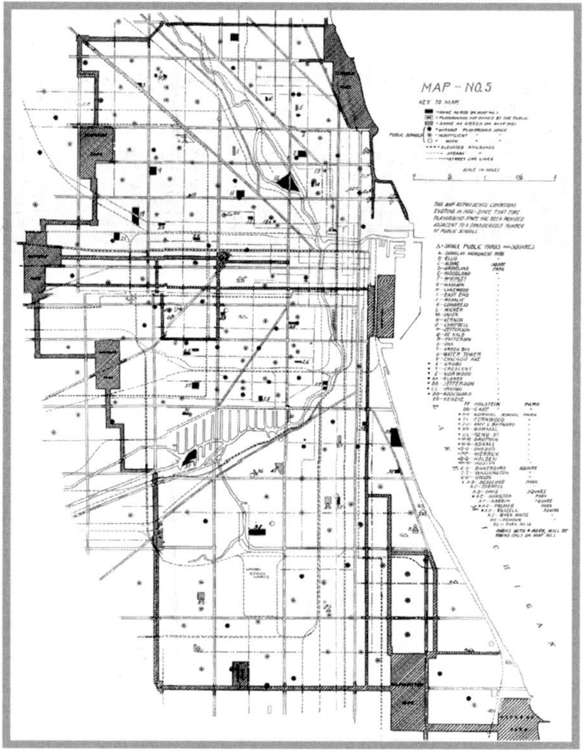
MAP — NO.5
KEY TO MAP

NOSTALGIC VIEWS OF

CHICAGO

ISBN 1-58973-003-8

Library of Congress control number: 2005933188

Published by Arcadia Publishing for Borders Group, Inc.
Visit us on the internet at www.arcadiapublishing.com

CONTENTS

INTRODUCTION

Chicago is known throughout the world for its architecture. Although many people are familiar with the city's skyscrapers and public buildings, they often overlook or are unaware of the mansions located throughout the city. These mansions represent Chicago's past and its future, and it can even be said that they are the very embodiment of Chicago and its architecture. The fashionable residences were built to make a statement, and what better way to have done this than to employ the leading architects of the time to design them. Men such as Louis Sullivan, Frank Lloyd Wright, Henry Hobson Richardson, Daniel Burnham, and John Wellborn Root all left their marks here.

Chicago is also a city filled with history. In nearly every neighborhood, monuments, markers, and memorials have been erected to commemorate this history. It is safe to say that Chicago has one of the richest collections of such commemorations to be found anywhere in the world. While many of these works were completed by local or virtually unknown artists, others were created by world renowned artists, architects, and sculptors including Pablo Picasso, Lorado Taft, Louis Sullivan, and Augustus Saint-Gaudens. Whether they commemorate events like the Haymarket Riot, captains of industry like Marshall Field, sports heroes like Michael Jordan, or famous politicians like early Chicago Mayor John Wentworth, each of Chicago's monuments, markers, and memorials has an interesting story to tell.

Finally, No other city in the world has a park system as great as Chicago's, which includes over 550 parks totaling more than 7,000 acres. The parks range in size from small tracts of land less than one-tenth acre, to giant parks measuring over 1,200 acres. Each has its own story as well as its own unique characteristics and history. Yet the great majority of us are not aware of the wealth, variety, and sheer number of parks that exist in the city, to say nothing of the ideas they project, the history they commemorate, or the manner in which they were named. When Chicago was founded in 1837, the city's fathers adopted the motto *urbs in horto*, or "the city set in a garden." Despite all the changes that have taken place since Dearborn Park was created in 1839, Chicago is still a city set in a garden.

ONE

HISTORIC MANSIONS

The Clarke House (located at 1855 S. Indiana Avenue and built in 1836) is the second oldest existing mansion in the city. It was built for Henry Brown Clarke (1802-1849) and Caroline Clarke (1806-1860). This stately white Greek Revival mansion, originally stood at 1700 S. Michigan Avenue on a 20-acre estate.

The Glessner House at 1800 S. Prairie Avenue is one of Chicago's most famous mansions, and it is an excellent example of Richardson Romanesque architecture. The home was built for John Jacob Glessner (1843-1936) a wealthy farm implement manufacturer. The architect of the home was Henry Hobson Richardson (1838-1886) who completed the design shortly before his death in 1886. The home, which was designated a Chicago landmark, is the only remaining example of Richardson's work in Chicago. The house is now a museum and open for tours. This is an interior view of the Glessner mansion featuring the first floor library. The library contains wooden beamed ceilings, a wood burning fireplace, Persian rugs, walls adorned with various paintings, and a large collection of rare books. On the large "partner" style desk, which was shared by Mr. and Mrs. Glessner, there is a death mask that was made of President Lincoln's face shortly after he was assassinated. Today the library looks almost exactly as it did when this photograph was taken in 1888.

This landmark Prairie School residence at 5132 S. Woodlawn Avenue was constructed for meat-packer and butcher supply manufacturer Isidore Heller in 1896. It is one of Frank Lloyd Wright's most significant early designs. This three-story yellow Roman brick mansion features overhanging roofs, rectilinear lines, large open rooms, three fireplaces, numerous windows for maximum light exposure, and a third floor that is decorated with sculptures by Richard Walter Bock (1865-1949). This home is on the National Register of Historic Places.

The Robie house at 5757 S. Woodlawn Avenue is considered by many to be the masterpiece of Frank Lloyd Wright's Prairie School style of architecture. Wright completed this mansion, which is famous throughout the world, in 1909 for bicycle, motorcycle, and automobile manufacturer Frederick Carleton Robie (b. 1876). The University of Chicago now owns the house. It is both a Chicago and national landmark, and tours of the property are available.

GARFIELD

The 33-room mansion at 726 W. Garfield Boulevard shown here was built for James Patrick O'Leary (1862-1925). "Big Jim" O'Leary was the gambling kingpin of Chicago and the son of Catherine O'Leary (1827-1895) whose cow allegedly kicked over the lantern that started the Great Chicago Fire. The home was designed in 1901 by architect Zachary Taylor Davis (1872-1946), who is better known for his designs of Wrigley Field and the old Comiskey Park.

This Richardson Romanesque Revival-style mansion at 25 E. Erie Street was built for Ransom Reed Cable (1834-1909), the president of the Rock Island & Pacific Railroad. Designed by the architectural firm of Cobb & Frost in 1886, this rugged stone mansion has been completely renovated and lovingly maintained.

This three-story Italianate-style sandstone mansion at 40 E. Erie Street was built for Chicago banker Samuel Mayo Nickerson (1830-1914). Designed by the architectural firm of Burling & Whitehouse, construction began on the mansion in 1881 and was completed in 1883. The interior of the 30 room Nickerson mansion is filled with alabaster, onyx, and at least twenty-seven varieties of marble. To support this massive weight, two-foot thick load bearing walls were used and a special reinforced foundation had to be created. This photograph of the grand entrance hall dates back to the early 1880s. This home, which is often referred to as the "marble mansion," was designated a Chicago landmark on September 28, 1977.

The Charnley House at 1365 N. Astor Street is widely recognized as one of the most significant works of modern architecture in the world. The house was built in 1892 by Adler & Sullivan, but designed chiefly by Frank Lloyd Wright who was a draftsman and designer in Louis Sullivan's office. It is a rare example of a design completed by both Sullivan and Wright. The home was originally built for lumber merchant James Charnley (1844-1905), but today it is the headquarters for the Society of Architectural Historians. The house is both a Chicago and national landmark.

Architect Stanford White designed the Patterson-McCormick Mansion at 1500 N. Astor Street in 1893. This four-story Italian Renaissance palazzo was built as a wedding gift from Chicago Tribune publisher Joseph Medill (1823-1899) for his daughter, Elinor, who married Tribune editor Robert Wilson Patterson (1850-1910). Cyrus Hall McCormick II (1859-1936) bought the house in 1914 and in 1927 he hired architect David Adler (1882-1949) to build an addition which doubled the mansion's size. In 1978 the mansion was converted into nine condominiums. This is a photograph of the front entrance courtyard.

Some of the most unique homes in Chicago are found on the 3800 block of Alta Vista Terrace. This narrow street just north of Wrigley Field has twenty row houses on each side of the block. Each house has an exact duplicate on the diagonally opposite end of the block. Architect Joseph C. Brompton designed all of the homes, which are 24 feet wide with 18-inch brick walls, in 1904. Nicknamed the "Street of Forty Doors" this tiny terrace became Chicago's first landmark district on September 15, 1971.

The Rath House at 2701 W. Logan Boulevard was designed by Prairie School architect George W. Maher (1864-1926) in 1907. It was built for John Rath (1870-1924) who made his fortune in the barrel making business. The two-story home with its low overhanging roof, and wide door and window openings is a classic example of Maher's Prairie School design. The mansion was designated a Chicago landmark on December 1, 1993.

This two-story Prairie-style Roman brick and limestone mansion at 5840 W. Midway Park was built for veneer manufacturer Frederick C. Beeson in 1901. It was one of several homes built for Beeson by architect Frederick R. Schock (1854-1931). Schock was a prominent architect in Chicago, but his most famous works were found here in the Austin community. Features of this home include a rounded second floor bay, hipped roof, and front entrance urns.

Sandwiched between two apartment buildings is this wood and stucco Prairie style home at 42 N. Central Avenue. It was built for printing press manufacturer J. J. Walser Jr. (1878-1921). Frank Lloyd Wright (1867-1959) designed the mansion in 1903, and it was designated a Chicago landmark in 1984. Over the years there have been unsuccessful attempts to move the home to another location, but despite these efforts the structure has remained on its original site.

Built in the mid-1830s, this 20-room residence was said to be the first real mansion built in the city and the first house in Chicago to be built with brick. This home was built for early resident and stockyard owner Archibald Clybourne (1802-1872). The home was located on Elston Ave. just south of Courtland Ave. next to his stockyard. The owner died in this house in 1872. Clybourn Avenue was named in honor of Archibald Clybourne.

One of the most fashionable addresses in early Chicago history was a one-block stretch of 11th Place just east of Michigan Avenue. This tiny street was known as Park Row because it faced Lake Park, which later was renamed Grant Park. This enclave of Italianate-style brownstone mansions, which was built in the 1850s, was home to some of Chicago's most prominent citizens. The houses survived the Great Chicago Fire but were later demolished to make way for the parking lot of the Illinois Central Railroad station. This photograph dates back to the 1870s.

Built in the late 1850s, this was one of several mansions found along a stretch of Ashland Avenue near Union Park. This particular home belonged to prominent Chicago banker Leonidas Virgil Badger (1806-1895). His enormous estate took up the entire block of what is today Ashland Avenue between Congress and Harrison. Badger's neighbors included Carter Harrison, Henry H. Honore, whose daughter Bertha became Mrs. Potter Palmer, and Mary Todd Lincoln, the widow of Abraham Lincoln. This photo was taken in 1870.

Elegant horse drawn carriages such as this one were a common sight along Prairie Avenue in the late 1800s. This particular carriage belonged to wealthy lumber merchant Turlington Walker Harvey (1835-1909). This photograph was taken in front of Harvey's mansion at 1702 S. Prairie Avenue. Harvey was involved in many other commercial interests in addition to his lumber business. One of his ventures was the creation of a town south of Chicago, today known as Harvey, Illinois.

Chicago's "Merchant Prince" Marshall Field (1834-1906) commissioned this mansion at 1905 S. Prairie Avenue. It was designed by architect Richard Morris Hunt (1827-1895) and completed in 1876 at a cost of $2,000,000, an enormous sum at the time. This three-story red brick Second Empire mansion with its mansard roof was one of the first homes in Chicago to have electric lights. It was demolished in 1955. This is a rare photograph of the library in the Marshall Field mansion. The library featured a 15-foot ceiling, built-in bookcases with glass doors, a wood burning fireplace, a stained-glass window over the fireplace mantel, and six-panel double oak doors that led to the hallway. The room was adorned with paintings, sculptures, ornate lamps, Persian rugs, and a variety of Victorian era furniture.

This 30-room granite Victorian mansion at 3400 S. Michigan Avenue was built for wealthy dry goods merchant Emanuel Mandel (1844-1908). Designed by architect L.B. Dixon, the mansion featured a carved oak staircase, numerous onyx fireplaces, 14-foot wood beamed ceilings, a large conservatory, a music room, a ballroom, and a granite rear coach house. After a devastating fire, the home was demolished in 1958.

This imposing three-story Richardson Romanesque-style granite mansion was located at 4455 S. Drexel Boulevard. It featured two arched front porches, gently curved bays, and a large wrought iron fence. This fine residence was built for wealthy Chicago businessman Arthur Middleton Barnhart (1844-1913) in 1880. For many years the homes sat abandoned until a devastating fire destroyed it in 1963.

This is an interior view of Harding's castle, which housed one of the most comprehensive collections of old arms and amour in the world. The private museum contained a series of winding stairways and a maze of secret passageways. When Harding died in 1939 his museum was opened to the public. Later the contents of his incredible collection were bequeathed to the Art Institute of Chicago where they are still prominently displayed.

TWO

MONUMENTS AND MEMORIALS

There is probably no other statue in Chicago that has terrified children quite like Massacre Monument. This large bronze sculpture is the work of Carl Rohl-Smith (1848–1900) and was unveiled on June 22, 1893, in front of a large group of dignitaries that included many famous Chicagoans, U.S. Supreme Court Chief Justice Melville Fuller, and former U.S. President Benjamin Harrison. The photo dates back to the time when this work was originally placed in front of the home of George Pullman, near the actual spot where the massacre took place. It has been moved several times since then and is currently in storage.

THE FORT DEARBORN MASSACRE

Pictured here is a 15-foot-tall statue entitled Monument to the Great Northern Migration, which stands in the middle of a small traffic island at 2620 S. Martin Luther King Drive. It has been estimated that between 1900 and 1950, over 120,000 African-Americans migrated from the South to Chicago. This statue, which features a man carrying a suitcase and heading north, is a testament to that long and often difficult journey. The monument is the work of Los Angeles sculptor Alison Saar (b. 1956).

From its inception in 1865 until its closing in 1971, the Union Stockyards was one of the largest and most famous livestock and meat packing operations in the world. It is estimated that over one billion animals were slaughtered there, earning Chicago the title, given by Carl Sandburg, of "hog butcher to the world." Today, all that remains of the 475-acre complex is the triple-arched limestone entrance gate with its copper roof designed by architects Daniel Hudson Burnham and John Wellborn Root. The Union Stock Yards Gate is located at 850 W. Exchange Avenue. In 1972, it was designated as a Chicago landmark.

The Drexel Fountain was erected to honor the memory of Francis Martin Drexel (1792–1863). The memorial was commissioned by Drexel's two sons, Francis A. and Anothy Drexel. Located at 51st and Drexel Boulevard, it is the work of sculptor Heinrich (Henry) Manger (b. 1833). Unveiled in 1882, it is believed to be the oldest existing fountain in the City of Chicago, and certainly one of the most elegant and exquisite fountains to be found anywhere. In the year 2000, the fountain was completely restored and rededicated at a ceremony attended by Mayor Richard M. Daley.

Pictured here is a United States Army tank which is the centerpiece of the East Side Memorial Park. This small triangular park—found at the intersection of Ewing Avenue and Indianapolis Boulevard at 100th Street—was erected to honor veterans of the 10th Ward in 1979. The tank and the massive Chicago Skyway Bridge behind it also serve as memorials to the area's steelmaking industry. Before most of the steel companies closed down or moved away from this area, they produced army tanks and materials for bridges like the one seen in the background.

Pictured here is one of two Bison that guard the east entrance to the Humboldt Park Rose Garden. One bison stands with a lowered head, while the other stares straight ahead. They were created from models provided by sculptor Edward Kemeys (1843–1907) for the grounds of the World Columbian Exposition in 1893. The garden provides a colorful background for the bison, which were unveiled in the park in 1911. Kemeys is best known for his Lions which stand at the entrance of the Art Institute.

JACK BRICKHOUSE
HALL OF FAME
BROADCASTER
1917 - 1998
"HEY HEY"

This statue of the Hall of Fame broadcaster Jack Brickhouse (1917–1998) is located near the Equitable Building on Michigan Avenue. When this statue (created by Daprato Rigali Studios, Inc.) was unveiled on September 14, 2000, the ceremony was attended by Jack's widow Pat, Illinois Governor George Ryan, and other dignitaries. There was some controversy when the Tribune Company elected to place the statue in its current spot, rather than at Wrigley Field, where Brickhouse had spent many years announcing Cubs games.

The General John A. Logan (1826–1886) Memorial is found in Grant Park near Michigan Avenue and 9th Street. Logan served in the Civil War and in the U.S. House of Representatives and Senate. He is depicted holding an upraised flag as a sign of inspiration to rally his troops. The statue was designed by Augustus Saint-Gaudens and Alexander Phimister and was unveiled on July 22, 1897. This photograph, taken in 1900, features a group of Chicagoans who are gathered at the memorial.

The two lions guarding the entrance to the Art Institute are among Chicago's most recognizable and beloved sculptures. The lions were cast for the World's Columbian Exposition in 1893. In 1894, they were donated to the Art Institute by Mrs. Henry Field who was the sister of Byran Lathrop, an Art Institute Trustee. The lion on the north end of the building is said to be On the Prowl and the south lion is known as Attitude of Defiance. They are the creation of the renown animal sculptor, Edward Kemeys (1843–1907). This photograph, which features three young ladies giving one of the lions a bath, was taken in the 1930s.

There are several statues of Abraham Lincoln in Chicago, but The Standing Lincoln, which is found behind the Chicago Historical Society at Clark Street and North Avenue, is considered to be one of the finest works of famous sculptor Augustus Saint-Gaudens (1848–1907). The statue of the great emancipator was commissioned by Chicago lumber merchant Eli Bates, who left a posthumous gift of $40,000 in his will for the creation of the work. The memorial was unveiled on October 23, 1887. This photograph was taken in the early 1890s.

COUCH

The southern portion of Lincoln Park was once an old cemetery. By 1866, however, the cemetery was closed, and shortly thereafter all the bodies and markers were officially removed except two: the Couch burial vault (which today still stands in the southeastern portion of the Park) and the Kennison Boulder, which lies a little further north. At the time, it was determined that the Couch vault, at 100 tons, was too heavy and too expensive to move and since the Lockport sandstone blocks that support the tomb had been cemented together with molten lead, its safe removal seemed virtually impossible. The exquisite wrought iron fence and most of the trees surrounding the vault have been taken away since the time when this photograph was taken in the early 1890s.

THREE

CITY IN A GARDEN

This is a 1916 photograph of the outdoor gymnasium in Douglas Park. This scene demonstrates the success of placing parks in crowded districts, where neighborhood residents had access to the facilities for recreation. Parks became meeting places for athletic clubs and other organizations. In this photo, a group of men and boys are gathered to participate in gymnastic activities.

This is a photograph of Douglas Park in 1910. The occasion is the unveiling of a statue of Czech patriot Karel Havlicek (1820–1856). The unveiling was attended by a crowd of nearly 20,000 people. The statue is the work of sculptor Joseph Strachousky. It was removed from the park in 1981 and now stands near the Adler Planetarium.

This is a very early view of Jefferson Park prior to 1886. This is a typical summer boating scene in the park during this period. Even though the park has changed drastically and the lake has been filled in, the park is still quite popular with local residents who stroll, jog, and bike there. People who work in the area also frequent the park. It is located across the street from the Chicago Police Training Center, and close to several area hospitals.

The land for Franklin Park was purchased in 1911, and the park was designed by Jens Jensen between 1914 and 1916 as part of the West Park Commission's Neighborhood Park Plan. Originally known as Small Park #4, it was renamed in honor of Benjamin Franklin on January 22, 1913. This is a picture of the pool that was placed in the park during 1916, at a cost of nearly $60,000.

Dvorak Park, at 1119 West Cullerton Street, is located on the Lower West Side. It is named after the Czech composer, Antonin Dvorak (1841–1904). The land for the park was acquired on March 15, 1907. This is a 1916 photograph of the playground, which shows children having fun on the swings and seesaws in the park.

Eckhart Park, located at 1330 West Chicago Avenue, is named after Bernard Albert Eckhart (1852–1931). He came to Chicago in 1870 and founded the Eckhart & Swan Milling Company. He was also a director of several Chicago banks, an Illinois State Senator, Director of the Chicago Board of Trade, and President of the West Side Park Commission in 1905. This is a 1915 photograph of one of the park's swimming pools.

nce to Merrick Park,
848

This is an early view of the entrance to Merrick Park, located at 5458 West Kinzie Parkway. Charles C. Merrick owned the subdivision in which the park is located, and he donated the land for the park to the city. The park is known today as Levin Park, in honor of John H. Levin (1887–1971). Levin was a park commissioner from 1946 until 1969, and he owned Little Jack's restaurant at Kedzie and Madison Avenues for over 60 years.

This is a summer scene of the wading pool at Humboldt Park in 1916. This photo demonstrates how early parks were intended to be used by neighborhood residents who rarely got beyond the city limits. Outdoor playgrounds and swimming pools provided recreational activities that were previously unknown to many people who might have never seen a body of water or a blade of grass.

Seward Park, located at 375 West Elm Street, is named after William H. Seward (1801–1872). He was Secretary of State under Lincoln, and was seriously wounded by Lincoln's assassin, John Wilkes Booth (1838–1865). He recovered from his wounds and retained his position under the new administration of President Andrew Johnson. The land for the park was acquired in 1907, and the park was officially opened on July 4, 1908. The park's Prairie-style fieldhouse was designed by architect Dwight H. Perkins. This is an early view of a baseball game played by children in the park.

This photograph of Holstein Park was taken in 1916. Even today, this nearly 3-acre park is just as popular with neighborhood youngsters as it was then. There are numerous facilities for children of all ages including the original fieldhouse, a swimming pool, a wading pool, two gyms, a basketball court, and baseball fields.

In 1915, the West Park Police Force consisted of 132 men. (This group was separate from the Chicago Police Force.) During that same year, they performed a variety of tasks ranging from arresting 317 people for disorderly conduct, to returning 61 lost children to their parents, or capturing 15 runaway horses that grateful owners were happy to reclaim. Seven people were also arrested for "stealing lilacs" in the park.

This is a view of Garfield Park prior to 1905. In the foreground, these men are involved in playing a game of croquet. One of the park's most interesting features was this lush open meadow. Croquet parties, as well as picnics, and military parades once abounded here. It should be remembered that parks such as this one were meant to provide city residents with open breathing places that contained grass and trees as well as ponds and fountains.

Grant Park is named for the 18th President of the United States and Civil War General Ulysses S. Grant (1822–1885). The park is 303 acres in size and bounded by Randolph Street to the north, 14th street to the south, Michigan Avenue to the west, and Lake Michigan to the east. Because of its location on the downtown lakefront, the park is often referred to as "Chicago's front yard."

29TH ANNUAL FOOT-BALL GAME
ARMY US NAVY
NOVEMBER 27TH, 1926
FORMAL DEDICATION OF
SOLDIER FIELD
CHICAGO
SCORE
ARMY 21 NAVY 21
COPYRIGHT 1926
KAUFMANN & FABRY CO.
CHICAGO

Burnham Park is named for Daniel H. Burnham. Located between 14th and 56th Streets along the lakefront, and connecting Grant Park with Jackson Park, at 585 acres it is the second largest park in the City of Chicago. The park was officially named Burnham Park by the South Park Commission on January 24, 1927. Burnham Harbor, McCormick Place, and Soldier Field can all be found in the park. This is a picture of the 1926 Army vs. Navy game that was held in Soldier Field and attended by 110,000 fans.

This is an early 1900s photograph of the workers during the construction of Palmer Park. It took nearly two years to complete the construction of this 40-acre park. Holy Rosary Church, which still stands on the corner of Indiana Avenue and 113th Street, can be seen in the background on the left.

This is an interior view of the auditorium which is located in the Sherman Park fieldhouse. This photograph was taken in the early 1900s. The beauty of the building was reflected in its utilization of wood, glass, light, and color. Note the use of wood in the floors, stage, beamed ceiling, and paneled walls. Light is reflected from the chandeliers, windows, and open spaces, and colorful murals adorn the walls of the auditorium.

Washington Park, located at 5531 South Martin Luther King Drive, is named after George Washington (1732–1799). The park was established shortly after the Civil War and named in 1880, in honor of our country's first president. The park was designed by Frederick Law Olmsted and Calvert Vaux, and it contained every conceivable amenity that a user of a great park could desire. Pictured here is a man enjoying an afternoon of fishing.

Until about 1920 the lawns in Washington Park were kept trimmed by a flock of nibbling sheep. These sheep were quite fancy Southdown sheep. Numbering 68 in quantity at one point, the expansive meadow with its grazing animals gave the park a sylvan, or pastoral, appearance. This aspect of the park was soon discarded when sheep were no longer allowed.

Jackson Park, located at 6401 South Stony Island Avenue, is named after the 7th president of the United States, Andrew Jackson (1767–1845). The park was founded in 1869 and laid out in 1871 by Frederick Law Olmsted and Calvert Vaux, and was officially named Jackson Park on July 11, 1881. It was the site of the Columbian Exposition in 1893. The park contains three major harbors, a yacht club, two beaches, a former U.S. Coast Guard Station, the La Rabida Children's Hospital, the Clarence Darrow Bridge, the recently renovated 63rd Street Beach Pavilion and the Wooded Island.

This is a very early view of the beach at Jackson Park, probably dating back to the 1890s. Note the numerous small horses and buggies that dot the walk. Other people stroll through the area or pause to take in the beautiful lake view. This beach attracted many citizens on a lazy afternoon.

This is an early 1920s photograph of Navy Pier Park at 550 East Grand Avenue. The park was given its name because of its location near the entrance to Navy Pier. Today the park is known as Jane Addams Memorial Park. A monument to Addams designed by Louise Bourgeois was unveiled in the park on August 16, 1996, the same day the park was renamed in her honor.

KAUFMANN & FABRY Co
CHICAGO
21-491-1

California Park at 3843 North California Avenue is so named because the western portion of the park is located on California. The land for the park was purchased between 1917 and 1931. The McFetridge Sports Center is located in the park. William L. McFetridge (1894–1969) was head of the Chicago Park District and leader of the Building Service Employees International Union for 20 years. This is an early view of the swimming pool in the park.

Logan Boulevard is part of the original park and boulevard system, providing a link which connects Lincoln Park to Humboldt Park. The boulevard contains a broad center strip that is covered with grass and trees and is surrounded on both sides by elegant brown and graystone homes. This is a 1915 view looking east from Milwaukee Avenue.

This is an 1890s view of a football game on the grounds of Lincoln Park. Park commissioners had made an early effort to encourage the exercise of sports and games in the park, and as a result, diamonds for baseball and football as well as courts for tennis were marked out for the free use of the public. When the practice of setting aside part of the park for such use started, opponents complained that since Lincoln was a public park, it was illegal to have such special privileges. The right to encourage sports and games was not contested for long.

The Lincoln Park high bridge, also known as suicide bridge, was a popular park attraction for many years. Construction on the bridge began in 1893 and was completed in 1894. At one time the bridge enabled park patrons to cross over from the beach drive to the inner drive, and it also served as an observation deck. The bridge no longer remains in the park.